COOL CASTLES AND PALACES
BUCKINGHAM PALACE

by Clara Bennington

Ideas for Parents and Teachers

Pogo Books let children practice reading informational text while introducing them to nonfiction features such as headings, labels, sidebars, maps, and diagrams, as well as a table of contents, glossary, and index.

Carefully leveled text with a strong photo match offers early fluent readers the support they need to succeed.

Before Reading

- "Walk" through the book and point out the various nonfiction features. Ask the student what purpose each feature serves.
- Look at the glossary together. Read and discuss the words.

Read the Book

- Have the child read the book independently.
- Invite him or her to list questions that arise from reading.

After Reading

- Discuss the child's questions. Talk about how he or she might find answers to those questions.
- Prompt the child to think more. Ask: Did you know about Buckingham Palace before reading this book? What more would you like to learn after reading about it?

Pogo Books are published by Jump!
5357 Penn Avenue South
Minneapolis, MN 55419
www.jumplibrary.com

Library of Congress Cataloging-in-Publication Data

Names: Bennington, Clara, author.
Title: Buckingham Palace / by Clara Bennington.
Description: Minneapolis, MN: Jump!, Inc., [2020]
Series: Cool castles and palaces
Audience: Ages 7-10. | Includes index.
Identifiers: LCCN 2018053971 (print)
LCCN 2018058686 (ebook)
ISBN 9781641288606 (ebook)
ISBN 9781641288590 (hardcover : alk. paper)
Subjects: LCSH: Buckingham Palace (London, England)
Juvenile literature. | London (England) –Buildings,
structures, etc. –Juvenile literature. | London (England)
–History–Juvenile literature. | Great Britain
Kings and rulers–Dwellings–Juvenile literature.
Classification: LCC DA687.B9 (ebook)
LCC DA687.B9 B46 2020 (print) | DDC 942.1/32–dc23
LC record available at https://lccn.loc.gov/2018053971

Editor: Jenna Trnka
Designer: Molly Ballanger

Photo Credits: Jose Luis Vega/Shutterstock, cover; Dafinka/Shutterstock, 1; davidf/iStock, 3, 16; maziarz/Shutterstock, 4; PA Images/Alamy, 5, 9, 18-19; David Steele/Shutterstock, 6-7, 17; Samir Hussein, 8; Noeyedear/Dreamstime, 10-11; Pool/Tim Graham Picture Library/Getty, 12-13; Lefteris Pitarakis/AP Images, 14-15; Mark Thomas/Alamy, 20-21; kyrien/Shutterstock, 23.

Printed in the United States of America at Corporate Graphics in North Mankato, Minnesota.

TABLE OF CONTENTS

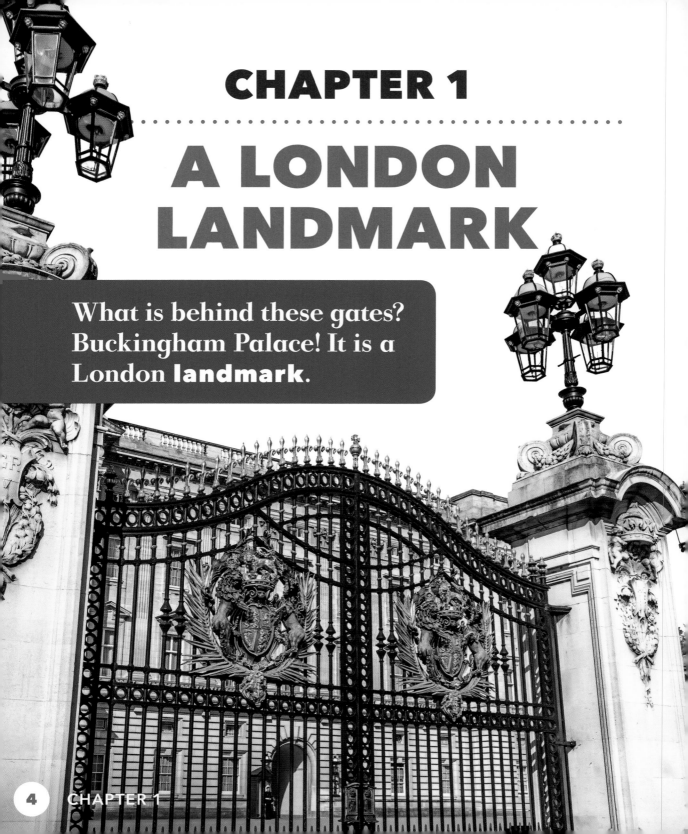

CHAPTER 1

A LONDON LANDMARK

What is behind these gates? Buckingham Palace! It is a London **landmark**.

Queen Elizabeth II

It is the home of the United Kingdom's **monarch**. He or she hosts many dinners and **ceremonies** here. In 2015, Queen Elizabeth II became the longest-**reigning** monarch.

This was not always a palace. It was first the home of a **duke**. King George IV ordered it be made into a palace. This was done in 1825. He died before it was finished. Queen Victoria was the first monarch to live here. Now, **tourists** can visit it. More than 15 million tourists come each year!

DID YOU KNOW?

During World War II (1939–1945), German planes dropped bombs on the palace. King George VI and Queen Elizabeth I lived here at the time. The palace was damaged. But the **royal** family was not hurt.

CHAPTER 2

INSIDE THE PALACE

The palace is filled with paintings. **Exhibitions** are held here. They show off beautiful items. Many are hundreds of years old.

Queen Victoria's Crown

The Grand Staircase is made of bronze. A glass dome is above it. Sunlight makes the staircase gleam.

Grand Staircase

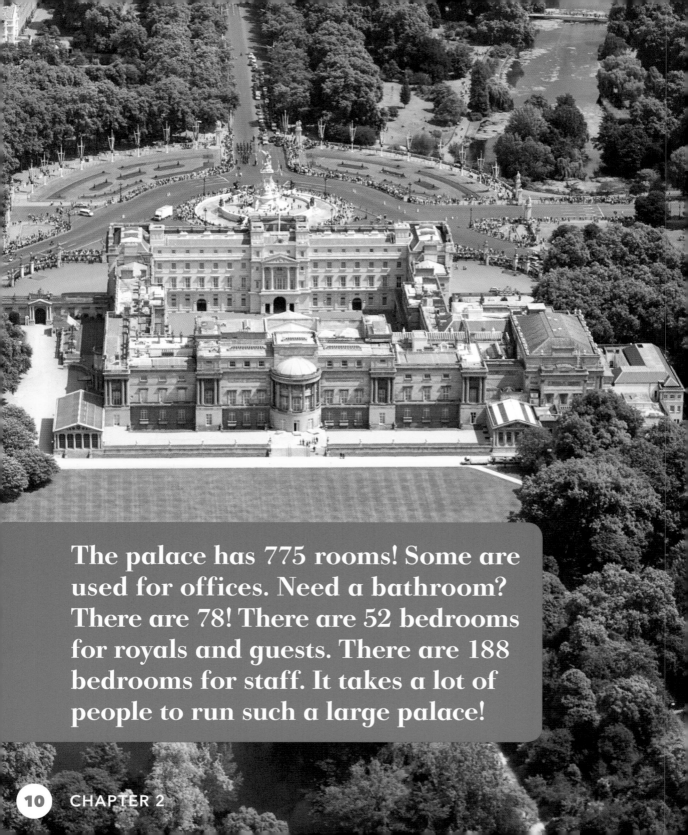

The palace has 775 rooms! Some are used for offices. Need a bathroom? There are 78! There are 52 bedrooms for royals and guests. There are 188 bedrooms for staff. It takes a lot of people to run such a large palace!

TAKE A LOOK!

Take a look at some of the special rooms on the first floor of the palace.

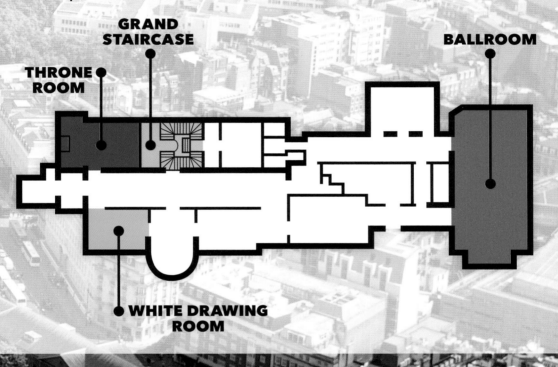

GRAND
STAIRCASE

BALLROOM

THRONE
ROOM

WHITE DRAWING
ROOM

Ballroom

The palace has 19 State Rooms. These are big rooms used for formal events. The largest is the Ballroom. This is where state banquets are held. These formal meals honor leaders from other countries.

And what is a palace without a **Throne** Room? Queen Victoria once held balls here. Today, the room is used for honoring people for their work. Pictures are taken here during special occasions.

throne

CHAPTER 3

A ROYAL RESIDENCE

Royal Standard

The **Royal Standard** flies at the top of the palace. What does this mean? The monarch is home! The Union Flag flies when the monarch is away.

Guards protect the palace and the people inside. Changing the Guard is when new soldiers come on duty. Bands play music. Guards walk in a **procession**. People watch. It takes about 45 minutes!

hidden
door

The White Drawing Room is used as a gathering place. The royal family meets here before official occasions. It is also where the monarch meets special guests. It has a hidden door. It is disguised as a mirror and cabinet. Royals enter the room through it!

WHAT DO YOU THINK?

Why do you think there is a hidden door in the White Drawing Room? If you could add a hidden door in your home, where would it be? How would you disguise it?

The royal family makes appearances on the center balcony. When? They gather here for weddings and **flypasts**. People gather below outside the palace gates.

Buckingham Palace has a rich history. Would you like to visit? You could see the monarch!

WHAT DO YOU THINK?

Members of the royal family have many duties. They travel to other countries to improve **diplomacy**. Some are in the **military**. Each member supports charities. Do you think these duties and acts are important? Why or why not?

flypast

balcony

QUICK FACTS & TOOLS

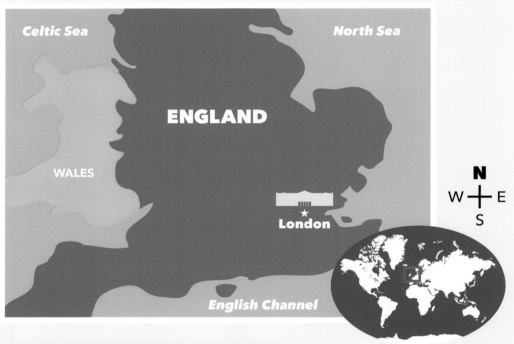

Celtic Sea

North Sea

ENGLAND

WALES

London

English Channel

N
W E
S

BUCKINGHAM PALACE

Location: London, England

Year Construction Began: 1825

Size: 19 acres (7.7 hectares)

Number of Rooms: 775

Current Residents:
United Kingdom's monarch,
members of the royal family

**Average Number of Tourists
Each Year:** 15 million

GLOSSARY

ceremonies: Formal events that mark important occasions.

diplomacy: The work of keeping good relations between the governments of different countries.

duke: A nobleman of high rank.

exhibitions: Public displays of objects that interest people.

flypasts: Flights of Royal Air Force planes that honor special events and people.

landmark: A building, place, or object in a landscape that stands out.

military: The armed forces of a country.

monarch: A person who rules a country, such as a king or queen.

procession: A number of people walking or driving along a route in an orderly way.

reigning: Ruling a country as a king or queen.

royal: Related to a king or queen or a member of his or her family.

Royal Standard: The flag that stands for the monarch and the United Kingdom and flies when the monarch is home.

throne: A special chair for a ruler to sit on during a ceremony.

tourists: People who travel and visit places for pleasure.

INDEX

TO LEARN MORE

Finding more information is as easy as 1, 2, 3.

❶ Go to www.factsurfer.com

❷ Enter "BuckinghamPalace" into the search box.

❸ Choose your book to see a list of websites.

FACT
SURFER